DINOSAURS!

TYRANNOSAURUS REX
AND OTHER
GIANT CARNIVORES

by
David West

Gareth Stevens
Publishing

Please visit our Web site, www.garethstevens.com.
For a free color catalog of all our high-quality books,
call toll free 1-800-542-2595 or fax 1-877-542-2596.

Library of Congress Cataloging-in-Publication Data

West, David, 1956-
Tyrannosaurus rex and other giant carnivores / David West.
p. cm. — (Dinosaurs!)
Includes index.
ISBN 978-1-4339-4237-2 (pbk.)
ISBN 978-1-4339-4238-9 (6-pack)
ISBN 978-1-4339-4236-5 (lib. bdg.)
1. Tyrannosaurus rex—Juvenile literature. 2. Carnivora, Fossil—Juvenile literature. I. Title.
QE862.S3W468 2011
567.912—dc22
2010009604

First Edition

Published in 2011 by
Gareth Stevens Publishing
111 East 14th Street, Suite 349
New York, NY 10003

Copyright © 2011 David West Books

Designed by David West Books
Editor: Ronne Randall

Printed in China

CPSIA compliance information: Batch #DS10GS: For further information contact Gareth Stevens, New York, New York at 1-800-542-2595.

Contents

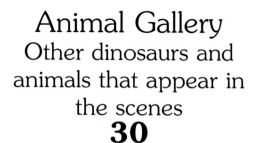

LONG TAIL
A long tail was important to keep the dinosaur balanced on two legs.

SKIN
Like all dinosaurs these giants had reptile-like, scaly skin. We don't know what colors they were, but they probably would have had some form of camouflage pattern.

This is Skorpiovenator, a giant carnivorous dinosaur from the Upper Cretaceous period of Argentina.

What Is a Giant Carnivore Dinosaur?

Giant **carnivorous** dinosaurs were large, meat-eating dinosaurs. They were the top **predators** and ranged in size from half a ton (0.4 metric tons) to a massive 8 tons (7.2 metric tons). They walked on two legs and had large skulls, with powerful jaws filled with sharp teeth. They used these weapons to kill and eat their prey.

CLAWS
Large claws on their feet made **formidable** weapons.

*Dinosaurs lived throughout the Mesozoic Era, which is divided into three periods, shown here. It is sometimes called the Age of the Reptiles. Dinosaurs first appeared in the Upper Triassic period and died out during a **mass extinction event** 65 million years ago.*

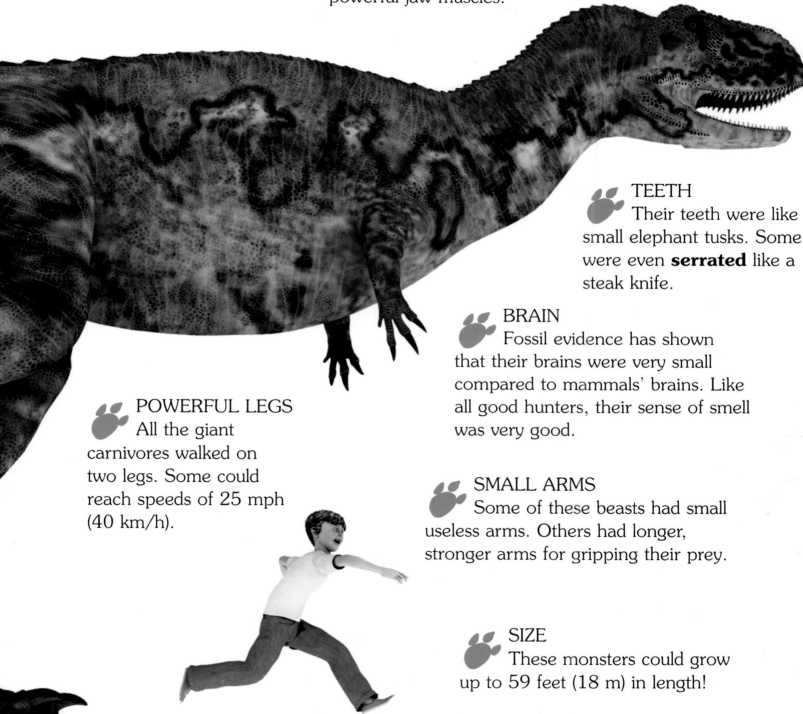

SPINES
Some giant carnivores had spines and sails sticking out of their backs.

HEAD
The heads of these dinosaurs were large, with powerful jaw muscles.

EYES
Like predators today, most of these killers had eyes that looked forward to give **binocular** vision.

TEETH
Their teeth were like small elephant tusks. Some were even **serrated** like a steak knife.

BRAIN
Fossil evidence has shown that their brains were very small compared to mammals' brains. Like all good hunters, their sense of smell was very good.

POWERFUL LEGS
All the giant carnivores walked on two legs. Some could reach speeds of 25 mph (40 km/h).

SMALL ARMS
Some of these beasts had small useless arms. Others had longer, stronger arms for gripping their prey.

SIZE
These monsters could grow up to 59 feet (18 m) in length!

	227	205	180	159	144		98		65 *Millions of years ago (mya)*
	Upper	*Lower*	*Middle*	*Upper*		*Lower*		*Upper*	
	TRIASSIC		*JURASSIC*			*CRETACEOUS*			

Abelisaurus

Abelisaurus was named after Roberto Abel, who discovered it. Many other **abelisaurids** have since been discovered, including *Aucasaurus, Carnotaurus,* and *Majungasaurus.*

Abelisaurus was a fierce predator. It had a large head with a rough area on the top of its nose. It walked on two powerful legs and probably had small arms. Scientists believe that having small arms that weighed very little helped the dinosaur balance on two legs.

6

A lone Abelisaurus *surprises a group of plant-eating* Secernosauruses *and manages to grab one of them in this scene from Upper Cretaceous Argentina. One of these hadrosaurs is only a small snack for this giant meat eater.*

It was big enough to prey on the young and sick of the giant **sauropods** that lived in South America. These sauropods, such as *Antarctosaurus*, may have been over 60 feet (18 m) long. *Abelisaurus* was also a scavenger, feeding on the corpses of dead dinosaurs and big enough to steal the kills from smaller meat eaters. It may also have preyed on smaller plant-eating **hadrosaurs** such as *Secernosaurus*.

Abelisaurus was about 30 feet (9 m) long and would have weighed around 2 tons (1.8 metric tons).

Acrocanthosaurus

Acrocanthosaurus means "high-spined lizard," which relates to the long bones growing from the top of its spine. Scientists think these bones were covered by muscle. This dinosaur is related to *Allosaurus* and is one of the largest meat-eating dinosaurs ever.

Acrocanthosaurus had a large head with powerful jaw muscles and a good sense of smell. It had strong arms to hold on to its prey while it slashed and bit with its razor-sharp teeth.

8

*A pair of Acrocanthosauruses **prowl** through the pine forest of Lower Cretaceous North America. They are quietly **stalking** a family of Sauroposeidons, intent on killing the young sauropod.*

It may also have used its claws to slash at its prey while holding it with its mouth. *Acrocanthosaurus* would have preyed on large sauropods such as *Paluxysaurus* or even the giant sauropod *Sauroposeidon*. These giant sauropods may have been too large to tackle and instead *Acrocanthosaurus* may have singled out youngsters to separate from the herd. They would also have hunted large **ornithopods** like *Tenontosaurus*.

Acrocanthosaurus was about 39 feet (12 m) long and weighed around 6.6 tons (6 metric tons).

Upper Cretaceous
76–74 mya
Canada

Albertosaurus

Albertosaurus was named after the Canadian province of Alberta, where it was found. It was in the same family as *Tyrannosaurus* but was smaller and lighter. It had distinctive triangular horns in front of its eyes, similar to *Allosaurus*'s (see pp. 12–13).

Typical of tyrannosaurids, *Albertosaurus* had small arms with two clawed toes on each hand. Its large head had powerful jaws lined with 35 sharp teeth. When it lost a tooth, a new one would grow in its place.

10

In search of prey, a pack of Albertosauruses *trudge across a dried-up riverbed during a drought. Many* **fossil** *skeletons have been found together, suggesting that* Albertosaurus *may have lived and hunted in packs.*

Albertosaurus had longer legs than *Tyrannosaurus* and was probably quick on its feet. Scientists think it could run up to 25 mph (40 km/h). This, coupled with its powerful build, made *Albertosaurus* a very fierce hunter. Its main prey would have been hadrosaurs such as *Edmontosaurus* but, as the top predator, it would also have taken the kills of lesser predators such as **troodontids** and **dromaeosaurids**.

Albertosaurus grew up to 29.5 feet (9 m) long and weighed around 1.4 tons (1.3 metric tons).

11

Allosaurus

Allosaurus, meaning "strange lizard," was a large **predatory** dinosaur that lived during the Upper Jurassic period. Its had two bony horns over its eyes, which may have helped protect its eyes in combat.

These swift, two-legged carnivores were both hunters and scavengers. They were the largest predators of their time and would steal a meal from smaller dinosaurs who had just made a kill, as well as hunt big prey. *Allosaurus* had weak jaw muscles. Rather than bite, it used its

12

An Allosaurus attacks a young Stegosaurus. A second, larger Allosaurus waits nearby, ready to move in to steal the kill, especially if the attacker is injured. (A fossil tailbone from an Allosaurus revealed a wound from a Stegosaurus tail spike.)

sharp teeth to slash at its prey with a wide-open mouth. **Juvenile** allosaurs were lighter and faster than the adults and hunted differently. They probably chased smaller prey such as ornithopods. As they grew older, their bodies became thicker and they became less **agile**. Adult allosaurs were unlikely to get along with each other. They fought and may even have fed on other injured allosaurs.

Allosaurus could grow up to 39 feet (12 m) long and would have weighed around 2.5 tons (2.3 metric tons).

Upper Jurassic
150–144 mya
United States, Tanzania

Ceratosaurus

Ceratosaurus, "horned lizard," was the only **theropod** with a horn on its nose. The horn was not used as a weapon and was probably for display. It may have been brightly colored to **compete** with other male ceratosaurs during the mating season.

Ceratosaurus had powerful jaws with enormous bladelike teeth. It used these to slash at its prey's flesh until the victim died from **trauma** and loss of blood. Its arms were short but strong, with four-fingered hands.

14

A juvenile Stegosaurus *struggles to free itself as a* Ceratosaurus *closes in for the kill. Both juvenile and mother* Stegosauruses *became trapped as they fell through the baked crust of a lake's muddy shore. The* Ceratosaurus *is too light to break the crust.*

Ceratosaurus had a more flexible tail than other carnivores. This might have enabled it to swim like a crocodile. If this was the case, it could have hunted aquatic reptiles and fish as well as dinosaurs such as *Camptosaurus* and the young of *Stegosaurus* and *Diplodocus*. Although it was smaller than other giant carnivores, it was able to compete with them for food.

Ceratosaurus grew up to 20 feet (6 m) long, and weighed up to 1 ton (0.9 metric ton).

15

Upper Cretaceous
99–94 mya
Morocco

Deltadromeus

Deltadromeus, meaning "delta runner," was a large carnivore that had long, unusually slender legs for its size, suggesting that it was a swift runner. Although it was a giant meat eater, it was very slight and was probably very agile.

Deltadromeus may have lived in mangrove forests alongside the giant meat eater *Carcharodontosaurus* and the even larger *Spinosaurus* (see pp. 22–23).

*On the flats of a northern African coast, a **pterosaur** makes its escape just in time as a large, speeding Deltadromeus lunges after it. Pterosaur fossils have been found with dinosaur teeth marks, suggesting that they were preyed upon.*

Deltadromeus would have been a formidable predator. Its jaws were packed with numerous thin, serrated teeth. These were used for stripping the flesh from its prey rather than crushing the bone. If a tooth fell out, another would grow in its place. *Deltadromeus* would have preyed on a variety of animals, from crocodiles and turtles to pterosaurs and plant-eating dinosaurs.

Deltadromeus was about 27 feet (8 m) long and weighed around 3.5 tons (3.2 metric tons).

Majungasaurus

Majungasaurus was named after the place where it was found, Mahajanga, Madagascar. The skull fossils were so well preserved that scientists have been able to make detailed studies, even of its brain, which wasn't very big.

This medium-sized carnivore had an unusual head. It had a short snout and very thick, roughened bone on top of its head, from which grew a small, rounded horn. Its jaws had a powerful bite and were crammed with more teeth than those of most abelisaurids.

18

A pair of Majungasauruses *fight to the death as a third looks on. If one is badly injured, it may have to give up. The winner will eat the loser—fossil evidence has shown that* Majungasurus *ate its own kind.*

Unlike most other large carnivores, *Majungasaurus* did not use a slashing blow to attack its prey. Scientists think it bit once and held on until its intended meal stopped struggling. *Majungasaurus* had shorter, stockier legs and a more powerful build than other theropods. This meant that even though it could not run fast, its strength was an advantage when taking on large prey such as *Rapetosaurus*.

Majungasaurus was about 19.5 feet (6 m) long and would have weighed around 1.2 tons (1.1 metric tons).

19

Monolophosaurus

Monolophosaurus, "single-crested lizard," was named for the long, bony ridge crest that went from its nose back to the top of its head. It looked similar to *Dilophosaurus*, which had two crests.

Monolophosaurus's crest, however, differed in that it was hollow, like the **lambeosaurine** crests. The hollow canals in the crest led to the nasal passage, which suggests that *Monolophosaurus* might have made sounds, like a musical instrument, through its crest. The crest

20

On the bank of a small river in Middle Jurassic Asia, a Monolophosaurus *sidesteps the swinging tail club of a* Shunosaurus. *These small sauropods could put up a dangerous defense against a predator's attack.*

may also have been colored and used during mating rituals. When it hunted, this giant carnivore might have been seen prowling the shores of lakes and rivers of Jurassic Asia. Its prey were medium-sized plant eaters such as the **stegosaurids** *Chialingosaurus* and *Huayangosaurus*, and the **ankylosaurid** *Tianchisaurus*. It may also have taken old or sickly members of the sauropod species *Shunosaurus*.

Monolophosaurus was about 18.7 feet (5.7 m) long and weighed around 0.75 tons (0.68 metric tons).

Spinosaurus

The name *Spinosaurus* means "spiny lizard." It was probably the largest of all the giant carnivores, larger than both *Tyrannosaurus* and *Giganotosaurus*. Unlike these, it had long arms and fingers with long claws.

The large spines that grew from its back could be up to 6 feet (1.8 m) long. It is thought that these spines were covered with skin to form a sail-like fin. This may have acted like a radiator, to help cool the dinosaur in the hot climate.

A *pair of* Spinosauruses *wander along an African coastline in search of* **carrion** *and hunting opportunities. One of them has used its crocodile-like jaws to catch a primitive shark, which has slipped out of its grasp.*

Spinosaurus lived along shorelines with tidal flats and mangrove forests, alongside *Bahariasaurus* and *Carcharodontosaurus*. It had a long snout with jaws full of interlocking teeth, like a crocodile. It was probably an opportunistic predator, scavenging and hunting sea animals such as fish and turtles as well as occasionally feeding on sauropods such as *Aegyptosaurus.*

Spinosaurus was about 59 feet (18 m) long and weighed around 8 tons (7.2 metric tons).

Lower Cretaceous
121–112 mya
Niger

Suchomimus

Its name, "crocodile mimic," refers to its distinctly crocodile-looking snout. It probably used it to catch fish from the rivers and streams of the Sahara region of Africa, which was lush and green at the time.

Suchomimus's jaws were studded with over a hundred teeth. Although not sharp, they pointed backwards, which would have stopped a slippery fish from sliding out of its mouth. It had powerful arms, with a 1-foot-long (30-cm-long) curved thumb claw on each hand.

*A Suchomimus out hunting for fish and other **aquatic** animals in an African river is taken by surprise by the giant crocodile* Sarcosuchus. *Although similar in size, the* Suchomimus *is outweighed by 4 tons.*

It may well have used these claws to help catch fish. Large fish, up to 4 feet (1.2 m), such as the *Mawsonia*, provided a good food source for this giant theropod. It would also have eaten carrion and perhaps other dinosaurs, since it was the largest dinosaur predator of its day. Its only competition would have come from the giant crocodile *Sarcosuchus*, which weighed a massive 8 tons (7.2 metric tons).

Suchomimus was about 36 feet (11 m) long and may have weighed up to 4 tons (3.6 metric tons).

**Upper Cretaceous
74–70 mya
China, Mongolia**

Tarbosaurus

Tarbosaurus, "alarming lizard," was a slightly smaller relative of *Tyrannosaurus*. Its massive head had jaws lined with serrated teeth. It would ambush its prey, running a short distance before delivering a savage bite to make a kill.

Many *Tarbosaurus* fossils have been found. **Paleontologists** found that its skull and other bones had air pockets in them. This made *Tarbosaurus* much lighter than other giant carnivores of this size.

A small herd of Saurolophuses *scatters down a shallow river as a* Tarbosaurus *breaks cover and heads for one of the younger members of the herd.* Saurolophuses *were a main source of food for* Tarbosaurus.

Tarbosaurus lived in a humid flood plain crisscrossed by river channels in what is now Asia. In this environment, it was the top predator, probably preying on other large dinosaurs like the hadrosaur *Saurolophus* or the sauropod *Nemegtosaurus*. *Tarbosaurus* had long legs but very short arms, with two-fingered hands that were practically useless. Its long tail helped it stay balanced on two legs.

Tarbosaurus was around 33 feet (10 m) in length and weighed about 4 tons (3.6 metric tons).

27

Tyrannosaurus Rex

The "tyrant lizard" was the largest tyrannosaurid. One of the best known of all the dinosaurs, *Tyrannosaurus rex* was a strongly built theropod of which there were several subspecies, such as *Albertosaurus*, *Alioramus*, *Tarbosaurus*, and *Daspletosaurus*.

Tyrannosaurus rex had a large head with jaws lined with 6-inch-long (15-cm-long) teeth with serrated edges. It would tear chunks of meat from its prey and swallow them whole, and crush bones to get at the marrow.

A male Tyrannosaurus rex prepares to back off from its meal of a young Parasaurolophus as a large female Tyrannosaurus rex charges in to claim the kill. Tyrannosaurus rex had a very good sense of smell and could smell carrion from a long way off.

Its two-fingered hands were joined to small arms, which it might have used to hold on to its meal. Like all large carnivores, *Tyrannosaurus rex* was both a predator and a scavenger. Although its top running speed might have been only 11 mph (18 km/h), it may have been fast enough to prey on large hadrosaurs and **ceratopsians**. Evidence of wounds on a *Triceratops* fossil suggests that it had been attacked by a *Tyrannosaurus rex*.

Tyrannosaurus rex grew up to 39 feet (12 m) long and weighed around 7.5 tons (6.8 metric tons).

Animal Gallery

Other dinosaurs and animals that appear in the scenes.

Secernosaurus (pp. 6–7)
"severed lizard"
Hadrosaur (duck-billed dinosaur)
Upper Cretaceous
Argentina

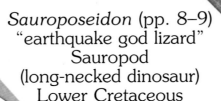

Sauroposeidon (pp. 8–9)
"earthquake god lizard"
Sauropod
(long-necked dinosaur)
Lower Cretaceous
United States

Azhdarchid
pterosaur (pp.16–17)
Pterosaur (flying reptile)
Upper Cretaceous
Nigeria

Shunosaurus (pp. 20–21)
"lizard from Shu"
Sauropod (long-necked dinosaur)
Middle Jurassic
China

Stegosaurus (pp. 12–15)
"roof lizard"
Stegasaurid (plated dinosaur)
Upper Jurassic
Europe, United States

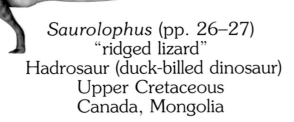

Saurolophus (pp. 26–27)
"ridged lizard"
Hadrosaur (duck-billed dinosaur)
Upper Cretaceous
Canada, Mongolia

Parasaurolophus (pp. 28–29)
"like Saurolophus"
Hadrosaur (duck-billed dinosaur)
Upper Cretaceous
Canada, United States

Sarcosuchus (pp. 24–25) "flesh crocodile"
Extinct ancient crocodile-like reptile
Lower Cretaceous, Niger

Glossary

abelisaurid A member of the *Abelisaurus* family of dinosaurs.

agile Able to move quickly and easily.

ankylosaurid A member of the *Ankylosaurus* family of armored, plant-eating dinosaurs.

aquatic Living in water.

binocular Using both eyes to look at an object, which gives good sense of depth.

carnivorous Meat-eating.

carrion The remains of dead animals.

ceratopsian A member of a beaked dinosaur family such as *Triceratops*.

compete To struggle against another for something such as food.

dromaeosaurid A member of a group of carnivorous dinosaurs known as raptors, which had big slashing claws on their feet.

formidable Causing fear or dread.

fossil The remains of a living thing that has turned to rock.

hadrosaur A member of the family of duck-billed dinosaurs.

juvenile A youngster.

lambeosaurine A member of the family of duck-billed dinosaurs that had hollow crests or tubes growing from their heads.

mass extinction event A large-scale disappearance of species of animals and plants in a relatively short period of time.

ornithopod A member of a group of bird-hipped dinosaurs that became one of the most successful groups of herbivores in the Cretaceous world.

paleontologist A scientist who studies the forms of life that existed in earlier geologic periods by looking at fossils.

predator An animal that hunts and kills other animals for food.

predatory The nature of a hunting animal such as a carnivorous dinosaur.

prowl To move in search of prey.

pterosaur A member of the flying reptiles that lived during the age of the dinosaurs.

sauropod A member of a group of large plant-eating dinosaurs that had very long necks.

serrated Having a row of sharp points along an edge.

stalking Following an animal closely without being seen, in order to kill it.

stegosaurid A member of a family of plated dinosaurs that included *Stegosaurus*.

theropod A member of a two-legged dinosaur family that included most of the giant carnivorous dinosaurs.

trauma A severe injury, usually caused by a violent attack.

troodontid Member of a group of small to medium-sized theropods with unusually long legs compared with other theropods, with a large, curved claw on its retractable second toe.

Index